Andreas Nauhardt

The role of pauses in speaker transitions

GRIN Verlag

Bibliografische Information der Deutschen Nationalbibliothek:

Die Deutsche Bibliothek verzeichnet diese Publikation in der Deutschen National-
bibliografie; detaillierte bibliografische Daten sind im Internet über http://dnb.d-
nb.de/ abrufbar.

Imprint:

Copyright © 2006 GRIN Verlag GmbH
Druck und Bindung: Books on Demand GmbH, Norderstedt Germany
ISBN: 978-3-640-44463-2

This book at GRIN:

http://www.grin.com/en/e-book/110260/the-role-of-pauses-in-speaker-transitions

The role of pauses in speaker transitions

by

Andreas Nauhardt

Martin-Luther-Universität Halle-Wittenberg
Fachbereich Sprach- und Literatutwissenschaften
Institut für Anglistik und Amerikanistik
Bereich Sprachwissenschaft

Wissenschaftliche Seminararbeit

Zum Proseminar „**Prosody in spoken discourse**"

Thema: **The role of pauses in speaker transitions**

Eingereicht von:

Name, Vorname: Nauhardt, Andreas

                   WS 2005/06

Fachkombination: LAS Englisch/ Sport   Datum: 23.04.06

Table of contents

1. Introduction

The following paper tries to analyse a passage of the conversation "Yum Chow" from *Wally & friends*. The presence of prosodic features within this passage which relates to lines 234 to 252 should be contents of this paper.

First of all, a definition about assessments including several examples and among others also from the datum should function as a first overview.

Secondly, there will be the transcript of the assessments and their next turns of the selected passage.

Furthermore, I will give a summary of the role of pauses in speaker transitions. This specific prosodic feature will also be illustrated by examples from the datum.

Afterwards, a brief summary of prosodic features in general should bring this paper to a conclusion.

2. Assessments

Essential to understand the role of pauses in speaker transitions, first of all, are background information and knowledge about assessments.

An assessment is simply an individual evaluation of someone else's utterance. Assessments are usually followed by agreements. Assessments are routinely used when people take part in social activities, especially in conversations.

It can be said that participation in events and assessing them are related endeavours. The example, which is given below and was taken from the selected passage, illustrates this point:

Example 1:   Wally & friends: Yum Chow (DAT: 28.01, 234-252)

```
1.  WA:      | | | ||| SEVENteen dollars is about twelve | | | ||| POUNds

2.  MA:      for the thr| | | ||| EE of [us

3.  BE:      [| | | ||| THAT's not dear
```

This example shows that an agreement follows an assessment. The assessment can be found in line 1 "for the thr| | | ||| EE of [us". It is a reaction to Wally's latter statement (line 1) and Mabel individually evaluates Wally's utterance. She offers further information. Within her assessment Mabel confirms and supports Wally's statement to emphasize how cheap the dinner at this Chinese restaurant really was. Afterwards, Bea responds with an agreement (line 3). She underlines that it really is not expensive for three people. Actually, it is an upgraded agreement. Later, upgraded agreements will be explained in more detail. Bea's agreement occurs immediately without any gaps or pauses.

Agreements usually follow an assessment but disagreements after an assessment are also possible. It is therefore of great importance what kinds of assessment are offered. Assessments are created as products for participation. That means that assessments occur as results of conversations. Thus, with an assessment a speaker asserts knowledge of what he or she is assessing. He or she is just stating his or her individual attitudes to the other conversationalist's latter utterance.

There are also different types of agreements and disagreements. As mentioned before, agreements, on the one hand, can be distinguished into upgrades, downgrades or into same evaluations.

Upgrades as types of agreements are characterized by a stronger evaluative term than the prior. Therefore, they increase and surpass the previous statement. Example 1 from above already illustrated an upgraded agreement. Another example should eliminate all ambiguities.

Example 2:   (Pomerantz, A., JS:II:28)

```
    J:    T's- tsuh beautiful day out isn't it?

→  L:    Yeh it's just gorgeous ...
```

L's agreement obviously includes an increase. The adjective "beautiful" from J's prior assessment is overtrumped by L's "gorgeous". Thus, it definitely is an upgraded agreement.

Another type of agreement is a downgrade. Downgraded agreements are scaled-down and weakened evaluations relative to the prior.

Example 3:   (Pomerantz, A., GJ:1)

```
    A:    She's a fox!

→  L:    Yeh, she's a pretty girl.
```

This example illustrates that L downgrades and devaluates the "fox-like-girl" into just a pretty girl. Therefore, L uses a marker in form of the preface "yeh" that indicates a disagreement. In this case it indicates a scaled-down evaluation.

A third type of agreement is known as same evaluation. In this type, a conversationalist asserts the same evaluation as the prior speaker's evaluation. Same evaluations are often indicated by "too".

Example 4:   (Pomerantz, A., JK:3)

```
    C:    ... She was a nice lady-- I liked her

→  G:    I liked her too
```

In contrast to agreements, certain delay devices are typical turn shapes for disagreements. One type of delay device is "no immediately forthcoming talk". Here, a conversant simply responds with silence to produce a disagreement.

Example 5:   (Pomerantz, A., TG:3)

```
A:     ... You sound very far away.
→      (0.7)
B:     I do?
A:     Ymeahm.
B:     mNo I'm no:t.
```

In this example B uses a silent pause, 0.7 seconds long, to indicate his disagreement that he expresses with "mNo I'm no:t". He thus responds with silence in the course of producing his disagreement to A's statement.

Another class of delay devices includes repair initiators. In this case, recipients request clarification with "what?" or "Hm?" questioning repeats. The following example will illustrate this point.

Example 6:   (Pomerantz, A., MC:1:30)

```
     L:     Maybe it's just ez well Wilbur,
→    W:     Hm?
     L:     Maybe it's just ez well you don't know.
            (2.0)
     W:     Well./ uh-I say it's suspicious it could be something good too.
```

There are even more possibilities and ways to express agreements and disagreements. The illustrated points should simply show the complexity and which devices conversationalists can use to agree or disagree with statements.

3. Transcript of assessments and their next turns

```
1.  MA:      so ||| ||| WALLy said WELL

             al||| ||| RIght THEN (.)

             so (.) w/ when we called

             for the bill it was ||| ||| SEVENteen ||| ||DOLLars
5.  WA:      yeah

    BE:      what's ||| ||| THAt

    WA:      and  [the headwaiter /

    MA:           <uhm>




1.  WA:      ||| ||| SEVENteen dollars is about twelve ||| ||| POUNds

    MA:      for the thr||| ||| EE of [us

3.  BE:      [||| ||| THAT's not dear




1.  WS:      [₂and the ||| ||| HEADwaiter brought it Over

             and i said it's my ||| ||| DAUGHter paying

             and he said of ||| ||| COURse (.) any

             when any ch||| ||| INAaman comes here
5.           he ||| ||| ALways expects his children to [pay

      MA:                         [((laughing))

      BE:                  [((laughing)) oh how ||| ||| LOVEly




1.  WA:      [it could ha/i thought it was very ||| ||| NIce

    MA:      [((laughing))

    BE:      [((laughing)) <oh>

4.  MA:      oh it really it really was it was super
```

4. Analysis of selected assessments and their next turns

Abstract 1:

```
1.  MA:      so |||||| WALLy said (.) WELL (.)

            al|||||| RIght THEN (.)

            so (.) w/ when we called

            for the bill it was |||||| SEVENteen |||||DOLLars
5.  WA:      yeah

    BE:      what's |||||| THAt

    WA:      and  [the headwaiter /

    MA:            <uhm>

    WA:   seventeen dollars is about twelve pounds
10. MA:   for the three of [us
```

This example illustrates that Mabel uses filled and unfilled pauses (lines 1 to 3) to keep her conversational turn and, of course, to keep suspension. In line 1 she uses at first a very short but a noticeable voiceless pause. After "WELL" she comes with another unfilled pause to keep the suspension once more. In addition, she makes use of another unfilled pause (line 2) and then goes on with her statement. To emphasize how cheap the dinner was and to get more attention she gets louder and stresses her statement in "| SEVENteen |||| DOLLars". Afterwards, Wally immediately agrees (line 5). While Wally continues talking, Mabel comes with a filled pause "<uhm>" (line 8). It is a hesitation sound and thus Mabel tries to maintain control of the conversation while thinking of what to say next. Obviously, Mabel succeeds in taking control of the conversation again (line 10).

Abstract 2:

```
1.  WA:      |||||| SEVENteen dollars is about twelve |||||POUNds

    MA:      for the thr||||||EE of [us

3.  BE:      [|||||| THAT's not dear
```

This passage clearly illustrates an agreement as a preferred next turn. First of all, Wally and Bea try to convince Bea of how cheap the dinner really was for the three of them (lines 1, 2) by stressing "SEVENteen" and "thr|EE". As a preferred next turn Wally, such as Mabel, expect an agreement by Bea. In fact,

Bea responds with an agreement indicated by an immediately coming utterance. There are no delay devices such as pauses between Mabel's and Bea's turns. In addition, Bea's agreement includes an upgraded evaluation to emphasize her agreement.

Abstract 3:

```
1. WS:      [₂and the ||| ||| HEADwaiter brought it Over

            and i said it's my ||| ||| DAUGHter paying

            and he said of ||| ||| COURse (.) any

            when any ch||| ||| INAaman comes here

5.          he ||| ||| ALways expects his children to [pay

   MA:                      [((laughing))

   BE:              [((laughing)) oh how ||| ||| LOVEly
```

In this selected part of the conversation Wally uses certain stresses to make his part or turn interesting. He thus tries to get attention and defacto, none of the other conversationalists interrupt him. Wally also uses a pause (line 3). At first, it is an unfilled pause to increase suspension but then this pause becomes a filled pause. Mabel and Bea simultaneously begin to laugh indicating an agreement. Bea even upgrades her agreement (line 7) "oh how ||| ||| LOVEly" to emphasize her excitement and to increase her agreement.

Abstract 4:

```
1. WA:   [it could ha/i thought it was very ||| ||| NIce

   MA:   [((laughing))

   BE:   [((laughing)) <oh>

4. MA:   oh it really it really was it was super
```

This abstract also includes typical agreement devices. Wally's turn (line 1) is followed by filled pauses and laughter (lines 2, 3). Bea also responds with an "<oh>" to emphasize her amusement and excitement. Both laughter occur immediately without a pause or gap what indicates an agreement. Afterwards, Mabel underlines Wally's statement again repeating twice how really super the dinner at the Chinese restaurant was. To emphasize her statement she even uses the preface "oh". Line 4: "oh it really it really was it was super"

5. The role of pauses

An important aspect for understanding the role of pauses in speaker transitions is the notion of preference. Preference refers to the customary and normative sequencing of conversational interaction that allows conversational interactants to make inferences about meaning. Preference functions as an interpretive mechanism precisely because, as in conversational sequencing, when a projected response is not forthcoming, it is noticeably absent[1].

Here adjacency pairs play an important role. An adjacency pair is a unit of conversation that contains an exchange of one turn each by two speakers. The turns are functionally related to each other in such a fashion that the first turn requires a certain type or range of types of second turn. This means that one turn is related in predictable ways to the previous and following turns. An answer follows a question in much the same way as an acceptance usually is given after an invitation.

It should be noted that not all invitations are accepted. However, in general, an acceptance of an invitation is what is usually expected. Therefore, two possibilities arise. One possible answer is preferred, that being the acceptance, and the other answer is dispreferred. This particular circumstance is known as the notion of preference. Some examples are presented to help illustrate the notion of preference in more detail. The preferred response after a compliment as the first turn is a disagreement while the dispreferred response would be an agreement.

Example 7: (fictional)

Disagreement as a preferred response after a compliment:

```
Tom:  Oh my Liz, your shirt looks really gorgeous.
Liz:  Well, I don't know, it's just an old washed-out shirt.
```

Example 8: (fictional)

Agreement as a dispreferred response after a compliment:

```
Tom:  Your haircut is beautiful, Liz.
Liz:  Oh, I know, I've just had my hair cut and I like it, too.
```

---

[1] Greenleaf C., Freedman C. 1993. *Linking Classroom Discourse and Classroom Content: Following the Trail of Intellectual Work in a Writing Lesson.*

Another example for the notion of preference is that agreements are usually followed as a preferred response after an assessment. Disagreements after assessments, on the other side, would define a dispreferred response. An example from the passage will clarify this point.

Example 9:   Wally & friends: Yum Chow (DAT: 28.01, 234-252)

```
1.  MA:    [for |ALL th[at we thought it would be |THIRty dollars

           [₁we |NEver thought it'd be seven|TEEN

    WA:    [₁yeah

4.  BE:    [₂yeah
```

In this example, both, Wally and Bea, respond with an agreement in form of "yeah" (lines 3 and 4) to Mabel's statement (line 1). Mabel obviously tries to convince Mabel and Bea of how surprised he was that the bill was just about seventeen dollars instead of the expected thirty dollars. Wally, who has also been at the Chinese restaurant, supports his wife's statement with his agreement "yeah" (line 4). Bea's respond to both statements is a "yeah", too. Bea thus agrees with Mabel and Wally and that is exactly Mabel's preferred reaction. Both reactions, Wally's and Bea's) occur immediately without any delays.

In conversation analysis, preference simply refers to a principle of making an anticipated response by the conversationalists.
One example is when an artist displays his or her work to an audience. In this case, typical responses are expressions of approval or praise. This would indicate that conversationalists are proffering some positive and honoured feedback. Yet, if there are no remarks of praise or approval the artistic may think that his or her works has been judged mediocre, unworthy or unimpressive.

In sum, if an action is orientated as an invitation it is called preferred next action or preferred turn. Its alternative is known as a dispreferred turn.
Concentrating on the shapes and nature of these preferred or dispreferred turns is the next part of my presentation. Here, the question of how these certain responses are performed is of great importance. Preferred turns maximize occurrences of the actions being performed using no gaps in between turns. Also, they contain components that are explicitly stated. This means that preferred turns occur unmarked in that there are no pauses and they take up the entire turn.

That is to say they are clearly identified. An example from the passage will illustrate this point.

Example 10:   Wally & friends: Yum Chow (DAT: 28.01, 234-252)

```
1.  WA:      | | | ||| SEVENteen dollars is about twelve | | | ||| POUNds

    MA:      for the thr| | | ||| EE of [us

3.  BE:      [| | | | ||| THAT's not dear
```

As mentioned before, preferred next turns occur explicitly and without any gaps or pauses. The example above shows that Mabel hasn't finished talking yet while Bea responds with her statement (line 3). As a preferred turn she takes up Mabel's entire turn. To make her assessment conspicuous and convincing Bea uses a stress at the beginning of her utterance "[| | | | ||| THAT's not dear".

Dispreferred turns, in contrast, minimize the occurrences of the actions performed by using delays and pauses[2]. This indicates that pauses in speech play a significant role. Dispreferred turns are, as a result, marked and implicit.
Some common techniques for dispreferred turns are prefaces such as "yes", "well" or "but".

Another important aspect for the role of pauses in speaker transitions is the phenomena of self-deprecation. Generally, self-deprecation refers to a person expressing a low opinion of himself in certain situations. The individual makes an assessment that is perceived to be a self-inflicted insult. Since the assessment consists of a self-deprecation, it requires a different and calculated type of response. The preferred response after such a self-deprecation is a disagreement and an agreement would be considered offensive.

---

[2] "Children's Arguing" (with Marjorie Harness Goodwin). In *Language, Gender, and Sex in Comparative Perspective*, edited by Susan Philips, Susan Steele and Christine Tanz. 1987. Cambridge: Cambridge University Press, pp. 200-48.

6. Summary

"Prosody, the rhythm and melody of speech", is important for extracting structural information and automating rich transcriptions. Past research results suggest that speakers use prosody to impose structure on both spontaneous and read speech. Such prosodic indicators include among other things pause duration and change in pitch range and amplitude."[3] Conversations typically include a wide range of these prosodic features. Especially, conversations with more than two participants, such as the chosen excerpt, are characterized by variations in pitch, loudness, tempo and rhythm. Loudness, for instance, can be used to express emotions like anger, to produce powerful effects, to drown other participants to convince them or as a device to target the utterance to proper recipients.

Duration of syllables such as tempo of sequences of syllables are other important prosodic features. Tempo of speech also frequently varies within conversations. Rhythm is also of great importance in conversations and plays a major role for turn-taking. Certain rhythmic patterns can initiate or end a topic or the whole conversation or just indicate the end of a turn.

This large amount of specific prosodic features characterize conversations and give possibilities to analyze and discuss among others the conversationalists' reasons using these properties. Thus, different prosodic features always occur and reflect the individual styles and patterns of conversationalists

---

[3] http://www.icsi.berkeley.edu/~yangl/word_fragment.pdf

7. Transcript of the passage

Wally & friends: Yum Chow (DAT: 28.01, 234-252)

BE: dinner table conversation between two older couples, Mabel and Wally and Bea and David. Mabel and Wally are telling the others about a trip to Australia and its episodes. Here they are reporting a cheap visit to a Chinese restaurant on New Year's Eve.

MA	– Mabel	WA	– Wally, Mabel's husband
BE:	– Bea, Mabel's sister	DA	– David, Bea's husband
Ruth, Vanessa – Australian relatives		Davina	- Wally's daughter who is living in Australia

```
1.  MA:   so wally said well alright then so w/ when we called

2.        for the bill it was seventeen dollars

3.  WA:   yeah

4.  BE:   what's that

5.  WA:   and [the headwaiter/

6.  MA:        [uhm

7.  WA:   seventeen dollars is about twelve pounds

8.  MA:   for the three of [us

9.  BE:                    [that's not dear

10. WA:   [and i/     [it was very nice

11. MA:   [for all th[at we thought it would be thirty dollars

12.       [₁we never thought it'd be seventeen

13. WA:   [₁yeah

14. BE:   [₂yeah

15. WS:   [₂and the headwaiter brought it over and i said

16.       it's my daughter paying and he said of course any/

17.       when any chinaman comes here he always expects his

18.       children to [pay

19. MA:               [((laughing))

20. BE:             [((laughing)) oh how lovely

21. WA:   [it could ha/i thought it was very nice

22. MA:   [((laughing))

23. BE:   [((laughing)) oh

24. MA:   oh it really it really was it was super
```

14

8. References

Pomerantz, Anita (1984): *Agreeing and disagreeing with assessments: some features of preferred/dispreferred turn shapes*. In: Atkinson, John/Heritage, John (eds.): *Structures of social action*. Cambridge: 57-101.

"Key words in conversation analysis". URL: http://bowland-files.lancs.ac.uk/staff/greg/key.htm   (7.12.05)

"Glossary of linguistic terms". URL: http://www.sil.org/linguistics/GlossaryOfLinguisticTerms/   (7.12.05)

Stephen O'Connell. "Managing Disagreement to Avoid Confrontation in Sports Talk Radio", Teachers College, Columbia University.
URL: www.tc.columbia.edu/academic/tesol/Webjournal/O'ConnellFinal.doc.pdf (7.12.05).

Cynthia Greenleaf, Sarah W. Freedman. "Linking Classroom Discourse and Classroom Content: Following the Trail of Intellectual Work in a Writing Lesson", Discourse Processes.
URL: www.writingproject.org/downloads/csw/TR66.pdf (7.12.05)

Jeffrey D. Robinson, "The Sequential Organization of 'Explicit' Apologies in Naturally Occurring English", Rutgers University.
URL: www.scils.rutgers.edu/~jrob/The%20sequential...apologies.pdf (7.12.05)

Anna Spagnolli, "An ethnographic, action-based approach to human experience in virtual environments", International Journey of Human-Computer Studies.
URL: www.psy.unipd.it/~varotto/diego_file/science.pdf (7.12.05)

Li Wei, „On the Conversation Analysis approach to bilingual interaction", Centre for Research in Linguistics, University of Newcastle. URL:
www.ncl.ac.uk/ecls/research/speech/publications/abstracts/liwei_langsoc_2002_full_text.pdf (7.12.05)

Eidesstattliche Erklärung

Hiermit erkläre ich,

Name: Nauhardt	Vorname: Andreas
Geburtsdatum: 25.05.82	

an Eides statt gegenüber dem Institut für Anglistik/Amerikanistik der Martin-Luther-Universität Halle-Wittenberg, dass die vorliegende, an diese Erklärung angefügte Hausarbeit mit dem Thema:

The role of pauses in speaker transitions

Titel der Lehrveranstaltung:

Prosody in spoken discourse

Im Semester:

WS 2005/06

selbständig und nur unter Zuhilfenahme der im Quellen- und Literaturverzeichnis genannten Werke angefertigt wurde.

Halle, den 26.04.06
       Datum   Eigenhändige Unterschrift